AN ATHEIST'S HANDBOOK

AN ATHEIST'S HANDBOOK

Dan Culberson

Copyright © 2005 by Dan Culberson.

ISBN: Softcover   1-4134-7653-8

All rights reserved. No part of this book may be reproduced or transmitted in any form or by any means, electronic or mechanical, including photocopying, recording, or by any information storage and retrieval system, without permission in writing from the copyright owner.

This book was printed in the United States of America.

To order additional copies of this book, contact:
Xlibris Corporation
1-888-795-4274
www.Xlibris.com
Orders@Xlibris.com
22391

CONTENTS

Chapter 1. WHO Am I? 7

Chapter 2. WHAT Do I Believe? 21

Chapter 3. WHEN Will I Die? 33

Chapter 4. WHERE Am I Going? 45

Chapter 5. WHY Am I Here? 55

Chapter 6. HOW Can I Be Happy? 65

Chapter 7. My Road to Atheism 87

Bibliography 95

Index 103

CHAPTER 1

WHO Am I?

I begin with a simple mythological, allegorical, morality fable and parable.

Once upon a time, a baby boy was born to a woman who was actually a virgin. The baby's father was a king, and the circumstances of the baby's conception were unusual. When the baby was born, an attempt was being made to kill him, but it failed and the baby lived.

After a childhood that we are not told about, the boy reached manhood and went to his future kingdom, where he had a victory over a formidable opponent. He traveled about the land and prescribed some laws for the people to live by, but then he lost favor with his followers, even though he was said to be the son of god, and he was sought out and driven from the city.

Our hero then met his death at the top of a hill, and although his body was not buried, today he has many holy sepulchres where the people worship him and his teachings.

Does the story sound familiar? It ought to, because it is nothing more than a generic retelling of any folk hero's life, using details listed by Lord Raglan in his book *The Hero/A Study in Tradition, Myth, and Drama*, first published in 1936 by Methuen & Co., Ltd.

In the chapter "The Hero," Fitzroy Richard Somerset 4th Baron Raglan (whose great-grandfather invented the raglan sleeve) lists 22 common events in the myths and lives of well-known folk heroes of tradition, as follows:

(1) The hero's mother is a royal virgin;
(2) His father is a king, and
(3) Often a near relative of his mother, but
(4) The circumstances of his conception are unusual, and
(5) He is also reputed to be the son of a god.
(6) At birth an attempt is made to kill the hero, usually by his father or his maternal grand-father, but
(7) He is spirited away, and
(8) He is raised by foster parents in a faraway country.
(9) We are told nothing about the hero's child-hood, but
(10) On reaching manhood he returns or goes to his future kingdom.
(11) After a victory over the king and/or a giant, a dragon, or a wild beast,

(12) The hero marries a princess, often the daughter of his predecessor, and
(13) He becomes king.
(14) For a time the hero reigns uneventfully, and
(15) Prescribes laws, but
(16) Later he loses favor with the gods and/or his subjects, and
(17) He is driven from the throne and the city, after which
(18) He meets with a mysterious death,
(19) Often at the top of a hill.
(20) The hero's children, if any, do not succeed him.
(21) The hero's body is not buried, but nevertheless
(22) He has one or more holy sepulchres.

Lord Raglan then goes on to apply the folk-hero pattern to a number of literary heroes and identifies the number of matches with each one, as follows:

Apollo—the son of Zeus, who was almost killed at birth and who is one of the most important Olympian gods of Greek mythology (11 points).

King Arthur—popular medieval legend and subject of modern-day Broadway musicals and films, who was raised in a distant land, won a magical victory, died by a conspiracy against him, was not buried, but has a holy sepulchre (19 points).

Asclepius—legendary Greek physician, son of Apollo and god of medicine, who was nearly killed at birth, his burial place was unknown, but who had a number of holy sepulchres (12 points).

Bellerophone—a hero in Greek mythology, who killed the monster Chimera with the help of the winged horse Pegasus, went into exile, and attempted an ascent to the sky (16 points).

Dionysus—the god of fertility and wine in Greek mythology and later considered a patron of the arts, who was almost killed at birth, went into exile, ascended to Olympus, and had no burial place, but numerous shrines and temples (19 points).

Elijah—Hebrew prophet in the reign of King Ahab and an outstanding figure in the Old Testament, whose body was not buried, but who had a holy sepulchre (9 points).

Hercules—most popular of the Greek heroes, who was famous for his strength and courage, who was reputed to be the son of Zeus, and whose body disappeared after his death (17 points).

Jason—one of the greatest heroes of Greek mythology, who assembled the Argonauts, searched for the Golden Fleece, and after his death was worshiped at shrines (15 points).

Joseph—the favored son of Jacob and Rachel in the Bible, who was raised in Egypt and wore the coat of many colors (12 points).

Llew Llawgyffes—a Celtic hero, whose mother was a royal virgin, who won magical victories with his father's help, and who flew off in the form of an eagle after his death (17 points).

Moses—the Hebrew lawgiver and the prototype of the Biblical prophets, who was almost killed at birth, gained a series of magical victories over Pharaoh, and who disappeared mysteriously from the top of a mountain (20 points).

Nyikang—the cult-hero of the Shiluk tribe of the Upper Nile in Africa, who disappeared mysteriously, was not buried, and had a number of holy sepulchres (14 points).

Oedipus—the hero in Greek mythology who solved the riddle of the Sphinx, married his own mother, was driven into exile, and also became known for the Oedipus Complex (19 points).

Pelops—a hero in Greek mythology, who was murdered by his father, served at a banquet for the gods, brought back to life, given an ivory shoulder to replace the one eaten by Demeter, and for whom Peloponnesus was named (13 points).

Perseus—a hero in Greek mythology, who was the son of Zeus, set afloat in a chest as a child, and aided by the gods in killing Medusa (18 points).

Robin Hood—the legendary 12th-century English hero who robbed from the rich, lived in Sherwood Forest with his band of outlaws, and helped the poor (13 points).

Romulus—the founder of Rome in Roman legend along with his twin brother Remus, whom Romulus killed after a quarrel (18 points).

Siegfried—also known as Sigurd, a folk hero of early and medieval Germanic mythology in the *Volsungasaga* and the *Niebelungen*, who became a ruler, but was killed after a plot against him (11 points).

Theseus—an Athenian hero in Greek mythology, who killed the Minotaur, instituted several reforms, and was rescued by Hercules after he was imprisoned in Hades (20 points).

Watu Gunung—a Javanese folk hero, whose life bears a striking resemblance to the Oedipus myth and who also goes to heaven (18 points).

Zeus—the supreme god of Greek mythology, who, after lots were cast to divide the universe and after the underworld went to Hades, ruled from Mount Olympus; was the symbol of power, rule, and law; and was the rewarder of good and the punisher of evil (15 points).

Lord Raglan doesn't include either Jesus Christ or You Know Who in his list of the Lives of the Myth and Famous, probably because even in this modern day and age, people are still afraid to offend the gods.

But what if "the gods" don't exist? What if God doesn't exist? What if all these thousands of years the human race has been treated like children by the priests and rabbis and other religious shamans just as parents have always treated their children?

"If you aren't good, Santa Claus won't bring you any presents this Christmas."

"If you are mean to your little sister, you won't get a treat before bedtime."

"If you don't do as I say, you are going to get a spanking."

"If you will stop playing and go to bed right now, you can have a special treat tomorrow morning."

I was six years old when I figured out for myself that Santa Claus didn't exist, but I continued to act as if I believed in the obvious myth and therefore turned the tables on my parents and essentially joined them in their deception in order to keep my little brother safe and secure in his beliefs of receiving presents once a year—as long as he was "good"—from a jolly old elf who lived illogically up at the North Pole. This also allowed me to continue to receive some free presents without having to do anything except allow my parents to believe that I believed and to continue their deception.

In other words, my brother would be rewarded as long as he did what my parents wanted, and I would be rewarded along with him provided I joined them in their little universal pretext.

What was in it for my parents? They could join the millions of other parents in the world and the millions of businesses around the world in this enormous deception of the children and the businesses' customers just for the purpose of enjoying a holiday once a year, indulging themselves in the delight of their children, buying their children's love with presents, and filling the cash registers with the parents' hard-earned cash. Oh, yes, and it also celebrated the birth of Jesus Christ.

What was in it for me? I got to participate in the bounty as long as I went along with the ruse, and I got to enjoy a tiny bit of satisfaction in the knowledge that I was helping my parents keep my brother misinformed for his own good, for my parents' good, and for my own benefit. I also got a tiny bit of satisfaction in being able to silently taunt my brother with *I know something you don't know!*

In other words, I had inadvertently become a priest of the religion of Christmas at only six years old.

And when my brother grew older, at some point he must have lost his belief in Santa Claus, even though it was never discussed, but our family continued to celebrate the religion of Santa Claus every year and exchange presents, just like all good Clausians.

And when I became an adult and was married in a church with the blessing of "God" through a spokesman and when my wife and I had children, we continued the tradition of the religion of Santa Claus, and every Christmas we all attended the Church of Santa Claus and gave presents to our children and to each other and perpetuated the myth that the presents came from the jolly old elf with the help of his wife and other little elves and eight tiny reindeer—no, nine—who all lived illogically up at the North Pole, all for the sake of the children and the parents and the businesses around the world who made a good living from the perpetuation of that myth. Oh, yes, and which also celebrated the birth of Jesus Christ.

It is a shame that the myth of Santa Claus doesn't include details of his birth, his lineage, and his lifetime struggles, so that we could see if he fits in the pattern of other mythological heroes.

Of course, the myth of Saint Nicholas the man seems to have helped it all along quite nicely, and isn't it convenient that stories and traditions that benefit a few people seem to come full circle without the help of any outside corroborating evidence?

So, who am I?

I am someone who as a child was taught an elaborate series of myths by my parents and by the society I grew up in, just so I would be good and do what my parents wanted me to do and act the way society wanted me to act for my parents' good, for society's good, and for the good of the priests, the rabbis, and the other religious shamans.

It took me longer to figure out for myself that God doesn't exist than it did to realize that Santa Claus doesn't exist, but I began to suspect it even as a teenager, even as I was attending Sunday school and church regularly with my parents.

I was a voracious reader while I was growing up, and I remember once when I was eight years old a friend came to my house to get me to play with him. However, I was in my bedroom reading *Riders of the Purple Sage*, by Zane Grey, and I told my friend that I was busy and didn't want to stop reading just to go outside and play.

So, when this book called the Bible that everyone believed was so important came to my attention, I determined that it was a book I had to read in order to see for myself what all the fuss was about. I decided that I would read it from cover to cover in order to learn what influence on my life it seemed to be having.

I read "Genesis" and was so bored I stopped reading after I had finished only the first "book." The Bible was the first of only a handful of books in my entire life that I started reading and couldn't finish because they didn't hold my interest. Not that it matters, but *Gulliver's Travels* was the second, also put aside unfinished as a teenager. I felt worse about not finishing that bitter and satiric masterpiece by Jonathan Swift than I did about not finishing the one supposedly by God.

So, I began early to question what made this ancient book so powerful when it couldn't even hold the interest of a curious teenager who found more joy in reading than in playing.

I remember thinking one day when I must have been about 13 years old, "God probably doesn't really exist, but if I ever have children, it might be a good thing to teach them about God and let them believe in God until they grow older and can think for themselves." Just like believing in Santa Claus.

The problem with God is that we can't prove that God exists and we definitely cannot prove that God doesn't exist.

We can only believe.

I am someone who began to believe when I was a teenager that God doesn't exist.

Even so, there was always a nagging fear that I might be wrong about this mythological figure who lived illogically up in Heaven, created laws to live by for the people on earth, rewarded goodness, and punished evil, and if that was so, what was wrong in covering all possibilities by going ahead and continuing to believe in God just in case God did exist and therefore my future after I died would be taken care of?

No. That was absurd. How could the very existence of one's being be so dependent on that individual's whim of believing or not believing in some other being's existence?

How could your future after you die be so dependent on whether you say "I believe" or "I don't believe"? That gives individuals more power when they die than they ever had in their entire lives.

How could the existence of the entire world be so dependent on whether or not we believe in God? That does nature itself a disservice.

If God exists, why is the world so precise and naturally predictable in its clockwork running? Why wouldn't God have made a world that requires more of God's intervention?

If God exists and even cares whether or not human beings believe in God's existence, why are there so many seemingly plausible and similar religions to choose from? Why wouldn't there be only two choices? God's religion and no religion?

So, just as I stopped believing in Santa Claus at six, just as I began to stop believing in God as a teenager, when I became an adult and had matured enough and read enough and learned enough, I became convinced that God doesn't exist.

And I was immediately at peace as such an enormous burden was lifted from my shoulders.

CHAPTER 2
WHAT Do I Believe?

When I accepted the realization that God doesn't exist, not only did I experience an enormous peace, but I also became angry.

I was angry that I had been deceived all my young life and taught to believe in something that didn't exist and that not only was not of any benefit to me, but was also a burden.

However, I was more angry that all of historical mankind and human society had been deceived by being taught and pressured into believing in something that doesn't exist for the benefit of the priests, for the burden of the religious subjects, and for the enormous suffering of those people who have been punished by the fanaticism of the terrorism and pogroms of religious fanatics against those people who were unfortunate enough to have been born into and raised in a religious faith different from the religion of the fanatics.

And the most anger came from the realization of just how easy it is to use God's name in order to justify anything that anyone wants to do. How often have we read about heinous acts committed by someone who used the excuse "God told me to do it"?

Consider how easy it is to justify to yourself to do something that society normally doesn't allow to the point that you can even believe that God actually ordered you to commit that act.

You might want something that you are not allowed to have, but you go ahead and take it anyway. Then you justify the act by thinking "If God didn't want me to have this (or do this) (or be this way), I would have been punished." Then, when you are not punished, your thinking can change easily to "God must have wanted me to have this (or do this) (or be this way), because God didn't punish me."

And then how easy is it for you to progress to the point where you simply think of something to do and the thought immediately leaps into your mind, "God must have spoken to me and ordered me to do this!"

The frightening aspect is that you can believe in the divine intervention with all your heart, simply because God didn't punish you when you committed the previous acts.

In addition, if you are in a position of dictatorial power in your religion, but you are afraid or reluctant to commit a certain act yourself, think how easy it is for you to take aside a follower who trusts in you and tell that person, "God spoke to me, and God wants you to do this. Don't be afraid. Trust me."

But if the person *is* afraid, think how easy it is to use the argument that can never be disproved, "Do not worry. If something goes wrong, you will be rewarded in Heaven."

However, what additional reward can be achieved in Heaven? You will live longer after death than forever? You will receive more bliss than eternal bliss?

In other words, I believe that all religion is based on fear and the fear perpetuates itself from beginning to end:

"I am enjoying this life too much, and I am afraid it will end after I die, because I don't know what is going to happen after I die."

"My life is horrible, and I am afraid that I will never have any relief, even after I die, but I am told that if I follow this religion, my life will be beautiful after I die."

"My life as a priest is easy, and I am afraid that if I don't continue to dupe the believers, they will cause it to end."

"My life as a priest is difficult, and I am afraid that God really does exist, so I must continue to encourage others to believe as I do, until directed to do otherwise."

"God is good, and I am bad, and I am afraid I'm going to be punished for being bad, in which case I might as well have fun being bad, because I am going to be punished anyway."

"God is good, and I am miserable, so I am afraid I must continue as best I can until God shows me the way to being good."

"I am afraid it is all out of my hands, I am not responsible for anything I do, and therefore I can do anything I want until God punishes me."

And finally, when someone realizes how powerful simply attributing any action to one's religion is: "I can't do this, because of my religion" or "I must do this, because of my religion."

The problem with fear is that it gnaws at people like a cancer and gives them an overwhelming need to control in order to overcome their fear, and eventually fear can cause them to become paranoid, as well as to hate everyone who is different from them and everyone who believes differently than they do. Their hatred comes from fear, and fear leads them to a desire to control in order to conquer their fear and to fan the fires of hatred.

So, what do I believe?

I believe that I should take responsibility for my own life, for my own actions, and for my own beliefs. I no longer believe everything that I am told by people who claim to have divine inspiration or who claim that God has told them something. I no longer believe in a religion that claims to be the only true religion simply because that religion has had millions of followers for thousands of years, simply because that religion has literature that its current followers believe was written based on the direct intervention of God and therefore is the word of God, or simply because that religion has inspired millions of people, thousands of priests, and untold numbers of buildings, works of art, and unsubstantiated deeds of wonder.

I believe that a fervent religious belief is another example of avoiding one's responsibilities, just as any other addiction is. Addicts are unable to take responsibility for their lives and cannot control their lives, and so they retreat into their addiction in order to let something or "someone" else control their actions, and thus the addicts (to cigarettes, alcohol, drugs, or religion) can feel good, knowing that they are being taken care of and don't have to be adults, to be independent, or to take responsibility for any of their actions. Religious "addicts" can turn themselves over to God or Jesus with the same abandonment to the "drug" of their choice as anyone does to alcohol or cigarettes or any other addictive behavior. They believe it can't hurt, and it just might prove to be helpful. Unfortunately, there is absolutely no independent proof that their religious addiction has any basis in reality.

I believe that the sun will shine somewhere tomorrow, but it might be cloudy where I am. I believe that the stars will shine somewhere tonight, but they might be obscured where I am. I believe that the moon will change phases every month in a regular pattern, so that we can predict what it will look like this time next month.

And how do I answer people who ask, "How can you look at the billions of stars and not believe in God? How can you see the beautiful, intricate workings of nature and not believe that God created it? Do you really believe that a more complicated Earth, sun, and universe could exist except for a higher power than ourselves?"

I say, "You are a victim of hubris and have an overweening pride and unhealthy self-confidence. You believe that just because *you* cannot explain something, that thing must have been created by an all-knowing, all-seeing, all-powerful supernatural being that you call God."

And to them I ask, "Why do you abrogate your own abilities and responsibilities without reasonable cause? Why do you listen to the scientific explanations for the billions of stars and still cling to your belief in God? Why do you hear the logical explanations for the past and present natural events and the predictions for future natural events and still deny what is before your eyes in favor of what has never been explained, simply because you desire to believe in the unexplainable spiritual reasoning that was probably force-fed to you when you were a child?"

I say to them, "You are another victim—'a sacrifice in a religious rite'—of a self-fulfilling prophecy. Once you state that you believe in God, you can use the excuse of God to explain anything you want: 'God did it.' That is a coward's way out of living. That is a child's way of living."

I believe that believing in God's existence seduces you into believing that you are entitled to something special or extra just because of who you are and what you believe rather than what you have accomplished. That way leads to "man's inhumanity to man," which "makes countless thousands mourn!" as Robert Burns wrote in 1786 in "Man Was Made to Mourn." A year earlier, the Scottish poet had written "The best laid schemes o' mice and men/ Gang aft a-gley" in "To a Mouse," and among the most famous of his poems are some addressed to a clergyman with whose theology Burns disagreed.

I believe that life is not "fair" and that people should not expect to receive special benefits just because of where they were born or of the color of their skin or of the religion they were born into, but instead should be treated and rewarded according to their accomplishments.

I believe that I can be at peace with myself and my beliefs in scientific explanations over spiritual explanations, because I am confident in my abilities to adapt to new situations. I do not need to be able "spiritually" to predict what is going to happen in order to be comfortable in my life. I do not need to follow astrology or some other preordained explanation of the way I am, so that I can give up responsibility for my actions. I do not need to believe in some being or beings more powerful than I am, who will somehow look over me and reward me or punish me, based on what I believe or what I do in the name of that belief. I do not need a parent to look after me anymore now that I am an adult.

I do not need to believe that someone else is controlling my life and that I am just a pawn in that spiritual someone's cosmic chess game.

I believe that I am an intelligent, confident, self-sufficient adult member of a society of similar and dissimilar beings like myself, and together we form a world community that best operates when it works together for the common good of the individuals and for the good of the community.

I believe that even though human beings are all alike, we are also all different. We need to be able to keep two opposed ideas in mind at the same time, because, as F. Scott Fitzgerald wrote: "The test of a first-rate intelligence is the ability to hold two opposed ideas in the mind at the same time, and still retain the ability to function." Consequently, we need to be able to work for the good of the human species at the same time as work for the good of the individual.

I believe that I can study the past, make observations about the present, and predict the future based on those scientific observations.

I believe that I can improve my current situation by being able to anticipate the future and to adapt to current changes, which is how the human race has been able to evolve over millions of years into its superior position over the other animals.

I believe that those who are not capable of adapting to new situations and being able to change will eventually die off, which is what happened to those species of plants and animals that have become extinct.

I believe that I should concern myself with my own situation and not try to inflict myself or my own beliefs onto others, because that way implies that I believe I am better than others.

I believe that I am a sentient composition of natural elements who is able to adapt to changing situations and who is able to be happy whether alone with my own thoughts and deeds or part of a crowd of others like me and unlike me.

I believe there is no one else like me and yet at the same time there are many others like me.

I believe that a slogan for good, healthy living is "Self-discipline with everything, moderation in all."

I believe that the Ten Commandments were an attempt to set down rules for people to follow in order to lead a "good" life, but upon researching them in both Exodus and Deuteronomy in the Bible, I discovered that they are not so hard and fast as we have been led to believe and they are also not so "Ten." In Exodus, Chapter 19, Moses returns to the people from Mount Sinai, where they and even other priests were not allowed to go "lest the Lord break forth upon them," and in Chapter 20 Moses tells the people what God had told him from memory, not with any tablets, and he recites 16 commandments. In Deuteronomy, Chapter 5, Moses gives a *different* reason why the people didn't accompany him to see God, saying that they had been afraid, and again he recites 16 commandments, I guess to refresh our memory, but at least they are in the same order as they are in Exodus.

However, I have to wonder about this incident that millions of people have believed to be true and literal. Why are there two different explanations for the same event? Was Moses lying in one? Which one are we supposed to believe? Why are the "traditional" Ten Commandments different from the way they are presented in the Bible? Where did the tablet or tablets that Moses was supposed to have brought down with him come from?

I believe that a happy and rewarding life can be fulfilled if we all follow the Ten Disciplines.

THE TEN DISCIPLINES (To A Happier Life)

1. The Earth is our home, which has brought us to life out of the elements of itself.
2. We shall worship no other spirits than the Earth, nor shall we damage the Earth.

3. We shall take time off occasionally for ourselves.
4. We shall work hard when necessary and play hard when possible.
5. We shall be kind to everyone and to every thing.
6. We shall not kill anything or anyone out of hatred or for personal gain, even when ordered to do so.
7. We shall be prudent in our choice of lovers.
8. We shall not take what does not belong to us.
9. We shall be honest to others and to ourselves.
10. We shall treat others the way we want them to treat us.

I believe in my own abilities, and I am comfortable.

I believe that God does not exist, and I am happy.

I believe that the more knowledge one has of oneself, other people, and the universe, the less need one has for a belief in God, "our Savior."

I believe that contradictions can live together in harmony.

I believe that I will die some day, and I am not afraid.

CHAPTER 3
WHEN Will I Die?

I have never forgotten a poem I came across in college while studying anthropology. The poem was made by an aboriginal Australian in the Australian variety of pidgin English and was recorded by William Harney:

> *"The god-men say when die that Jesus came*
> *To save our sins and let us know*
> *The right from wrong and in his name*
> *To die and into heaven go—*
> *Might be, might be; I don't know.*
>
> *"The god-men say when die go sky*
> *Through Pearly Gates where river flow,*
> *The god-man say when die we fly*
> *Just like eaglehawk and crow—*
> *Might be, might be; I don't know."*

The "god-men," of course, are not spiritual deities of the aborigine's religion speaking directly to the aborigine. They are Christian missionaries trying to inflict their religion onto the "heathen" whom they probably thought didn't know any better and must be saved by them.

When I reflect on all the damage that has been done throughout history "in God's name" to uncivilized as well as to civilized people, I have to wonder why any person—civilized or uncivilized, for that matter—would want to accept the beliefs of any particular cruel religion. Either the cruelty was being inflicted by grossly imperfect "missionaries of God" or else God was confident that those cruelties would be overlooked and new converts would flock to the missionaries' religion anyway.

Or else God doesn't exist, and the missionaries were nothing more than self-serving or misguided shamans who were afraid of death and desperately engaged in a self-fulfilling prophecy of their own making: the more people they can convert to their religion by whatever means possible lends more credence to their religion and to their own beliefs.

Consider one of the most visible arguments some poor Christian uses on Sunday afternoons for becoming a Christian. If you watch professional football on TV, surely at least once you have seen some lonely guy sitting in the crowd behind the end zone constantly holding up a sign that says "John 3:16" whenever an extra point is kicked.

Apparently, this "picketer" believes all he has to do in order to acquire more converts is to hold up his sign on national TV and people will flock to his faith.

Well, take some time to consider what Chapter 3, Verse 16, of the book of John in the Bible says:

> *"For God so loved the world,*
> *that he gave his only begotten Son,*
> *that whosoever believeth in him*
> *should not perish, but have everlasting life."*

"For God so loved the world": Does the Supreme Creator have emotions like love, hate, disgust, and boredom? To me, that seems to be a failing in an "all-powerful God." Is "the world" the entire universe with its billions of galaxies and trillions of stars or just the Earth on which we humans exist?

"That he gave his only begotten Son": There is that parent-child thing again. "Begotten" is the past participle of "beget," which means "to procreate as the father" or "to sire." Why is this argument supposed to be impressive? If God is so "all-powerful" and so obsessed with converting his imperfect creations to believing in him, why wouldn't he send down "begotten Sons" like crazy to do the trick?

"That whosoever believeth in him": Doesn't this point out another failing in God? If God is so obsessed with human beings believing in God, why didn't he just make them that way in the first place? And note that the lowercase "him" refers back to the lowercase "he" which refers back to God, not to the uppercase "Son."

"Should not perish, but have everlasting life": Aha! There it is. If you believe in God, you will not die. You will have "everlasting life."

Well, why would God make an imperfect world with imperfect people to begin with? Then, given that, why would he feel compelled to set up this test for people? Does he want to clog up Heaven with saved souls, or is he engaged in some diabolical contest with Satan, God's fallen angel, to see who is more powerful and who can collect the most souls? That doesn't seem very God-like, either.

No, John 3:16 seems to be just another argument from religious shamans to acquire more converts to the shamans' religion so that the shamans' future is secure: "Believe in God (and I'll show you how to do it), and you will never die."

Seeing and hearing things like people, signs, and bumper stickers that proclaim "John 3:16," or "God Is Good/All the Time," or "Jesus Loves You" only reminds me of frightened people whistling in the dark trying to shore up their own courage in order to help them overcome their childish fear of the darkness, the unknown, and death.

I can understand why people fear death. Life is so full and rewarding and interesting, and death, by nature, is not. Death must be like sleep, only probably without the dreaming.

On the other hand, if Heaven is such a wonderful place and if life after death is such a wonderful state to be in, why do we all spend so much time, effort, and money trying to avoid going there and being in that state? Why is suicide "wrong"? Why is assisted dying "wrong"? Why is abortion considered to be "wrong"? All of those acts are simply intended to help someone go to so-called eternal bliss and everlasting life.

Unless there is no Heaven, there is no life after death, and there is no God.

We can control what we do and say and think when we are awake. When we are sleeping, however, we lose that control and are at the mercy of our subconscious and unconscious selves.

Who hasn't lain in bed at night in the dark just before falling asleep wondering about what could happen without our knowledge while we are asleep? We become just a little bit frightened, because the world around us slips out of our control while we are asleep.

Who hasn't wondered about the possibility of dying while asleep and thought about everything in our lives that remains unfinished? We become frightened at the prospect of having failed to have led a complete life at the end of each day.

Who hasn't thought about death and wondered if death isn't simply an eternal state of non-dreaming sleep, an eternal period of the world going on without us to control what little part we can and have become used to, a world's lifetime full of people we know and people we love that doesn't include us? We become frightened at the thought of having the wonder of our life snuffed out like a candle in the darkness.

Then consider the possible logic of an early shaman who might have thought about death and the fear of death that everyone experienced:

"Life is good, and therefore death must be bad. When I sleep, I look and act to others as if I am dead, and yet sometimes I dream of beautiful, wonderful places and of doing beautiful and wonderful things. What if death isn't the end of life as we believe it is? What if death is really an eternal state of beautiful, wonderful dreaming?

"I believe I can convince my followers of this idea. I'll try it out, and if they accept it, that will give me even more power over them as I imagine this beautiful, wonderful concept of life after death for them.

"Who knows? Perhaps this idea was even given to me by the gods! If it is so, that makes it so."

So, when will I die? In the words of the aboriginal poet: "I don't know."

Am I ready to die? Of course not. Not yet, anyway.

Will I be ready to die when I am old and have lived a full life? I believe so, because when we are old our bodies are used up, and living then becomes more difficult. It is no surprise or coincidence that R.I.P. stands for "Rest In Peace."

Is the thought of death frightening? No more so than that tiny prick of fear I sometimes feel in bed at night in the dark just before falling asleep.

Am I afraid of losing the control of my life that I have become used to? No, I have realized ever since I became an adult that there are some things I can control and some things I cannot. Even though we fear what we cannot control, I don't fear the government, people in other countries, the world economy, the telephone companies, City Hall, or even my next-door neighbor. I also don't fear losing control of paying my bills, deciding what to eat for breakfast, or what to watch on TV. In other words, I do not fear what I cannot control, and I do not fear death.

Will I miss life and the kinship of my fellow human beings and the love of my family? Of course, but I can also imagine other people whose life is more difficult than mine and who might not have very many friends and supporters or family to help them through a difficult life.

For those people, Heaven could certainly seem to be a blessing to look forward to, if they can only get over that initial fear of losing complete and final control of their lives, that tiny prick of fear before falling asleep magnified a hundredfold—no, a thousandfold . . . . No, an infinityfold.

Why are we sad when someone or something close to us dies? Are we simply being selfish and mourning the loss of someone or something that *we* have lost and that will no longer be a part of *our* lives? Well, there is also the sadness that that someone or something is no longer living and therefore no longer enjoying the beauty and wonder of life, but when we mourn someone's death, do we think more about the loss of that someone's life that that person has suffered or do we think more about the loss of that someone's presence from our own lives?

I have experienced death many times in my life. When I was two years old, my mother had a miscarriage, but I don't remember it, and I don't know anything about it other than the few times my mother happened to refer to it over the years. When I was six, my brother was born, and there was no need to mention a lost child.

When I was 10, a teacher of mine died while she was on vacation, and I vaguely remember going to her funeral, but that is all. At about that same time, our dog Bingo was hit by an automobile and died, and I vaguely remember being sad for a while, but that is all.

Then, over the years there were other pets who died and left my life—dogs, cats, fish, turtles—and all I remember is a brief period of sadness, but that is all.

When I was 16, a classmate of mine died suddenly. I knew him and spoke with him whenever we met, but I didn't attend his funeral, and I don't remember feeling anything at all other than mild curiosity. That is all.

When I was 26, I almost died. I had a motorcycle accident in the mountains and 10 days later came to while walking down the hall in the hospital. I remember nothing about the accident itself, just the part of borrowing my friend's motorcycle after a picnic and starting down the road. The fact that I came very close to dying and would never even have known it made a strong impression on me. I realized that death can come at any time without any warning—such that you might not even know that you are going to die—and I came to appreciate life more and to respect death more. I respect death, but I do not fear it. That is all.

When my son was about five years old, his pet bird died, and he took care of all the funeral arrangements himself. He buried the bird in the back yard and painted an epitaph on a flat stone that he placed over the grave: "Here lies Fred. Dead."

When my father had a heart attack and my brother called me at work to notify me, I drove the 100 miles to my parents' home with my chest heaving while I fought back the tears that interfered with my driving. His prospect of surviving was not good, and I prepared myself for his probable death during the drive. When I arrived in front of the house, the next-door neighbor was at my car before I even opened the car door. She was crying and informed me that my father was dead, but I felt nothing stronger than I had already felt while driving down there. During the private viewing at the funeral home, my mother gave me his wedding ring to place back on his finger, and I looked down at his waxlike face, raised his left hand, and slipped the gold band over the still, cold finger without emotion. That is all.

Shortly after my father died, the baby son of a colleague of mine at work died in his crib. Not too long before, we had all attended a group dinner together, and the son had been fussy. I was the only one who could settle him down, and I picked him up and took him out onto the porch of the restaurant and talked to him and sang to him and tried to remember all the tricks I had used with my own son and daughter. The tricks worked, and the baby settled down and even went to sleep. At the baby's funeral, I felt sadness for his parents, and at his grave I tossed some wild flowers onto his tiny coffin. That is all.

The best thing I can do for my family is to make the necessary arrangements for my death so that they will not be troubled with those distractions during their period of grieving.

The best thing I can do for me is to prepare myself for an eternity of nothing after I die.

The best thing I can do is to treat the prospect of death like that little prick of fear I sometimes feel in bed at night in the dark just before falling asleep.

The best thing I can do is to remember the last line of that poetic aborigine's beautiful, wonderful poem:

"Might be, might be; I don't know."

CHAPTER 4

WHERE Am I Going?

"The god-men say when die go sky,
Through Pearly Gates where river flow,"

We are taught that one of the many difficulties of any religion's philosophy or messianic movement is making predictions of a nature that are either too soon in the future so that the date comes and goes without the prediction coming true or else too detailed so that the accuracy of the prediction is seriously in question.

"Pearly Gates" leading to Heaven "where river flow" is probably too detailed for a destination after we die, and both of those concrete details supposedly occupying space *up in the sky* might have caused the aborigine to question the sanity of the god-men preaching about the wonders of Heaven and about life after death and, by association, the wonders of the god-men's particular religion.

Of course, any prediction of where we go after death is fairly safe from contradiction.

Better that one should fall back on the words of Shakespeare's Hamlet and claim ignorance:

> "*There are more things in heaven and earth . . .*
> *Than are dreamt of in your philosophy*"

The biggest mistake with religions and messiahs and predictions is to predict the end of the world or the resurrection of the religion's leader after the leader's death. Then we get the pathetic results such as the ghost-dance song of the Arapahoe Indians in the late 1800s:

> "*Father, have pity on me,*
> *Father, have pity on me;*
> *I am crying for thirst,*
> *I am crying for thirst;*
> *All is gone—I have nothing to eat,*
> *All is gone—I have nothing to eat.*"

The ghost dance was a ritual that was central to the messianic religion begun about 1870 among the Paiute Indians by their prophet Wovoka. Wovoka predicted that pacifism and the sacred ghost dance, which was danced for five successive days and was accompanied by hypnotic trances, would cause the invading white people to disappear and that all Indians would have their land returned to them and they would be free from death, disease, and misery.

The ghost-dance religion spread to most of the western Indians, but after Wovoka's supernatural "ghost shirts" failed tragically in 1890 for the Sioux Indians at the massacre at Wounded Knee, the religion died out. The ghost shirts were supposed to protect the wearers from the white man's bullets, and there is nothing else like the failed prediction of a handmade shirt that will stop bullets to help a prophet lose religious converts.

The danger of any movement built only on faith comes when the shamans predict something that does not come to pass or make promises to their followers that do not come true or set up rules of conduct that they themselves do not follow. That way lies the Ghost Dance of Chrisianity, Judaism, and Islam.

Better that the leaders of any group of people practice what I believe is the way to live one's life: "Self-discipline in everything, moderation in all."

Wovoka's prophecies were too short-term and too detailed for the ghost-dance religion to succeed, in addition to being incorrect.

Of course, any prediction of what happens to us after we die comes down to a self-fulfilling prophecy that cannot be proven. If we believe in Heaven, then after we die, by God, we go to Heaven. If we believe that we simply return to dust after we die, then, by Gaea, we return to dust.

Proving what happens after we die is as difficult, ephemeral, and capricious as proving what we are going to believe tomorrow. We cannot prove it today, and tomorrow we might be lying. However, if some shamans can take advantage of the fears of death experienced by a band of people and profit from it as well, then, by whatever god the shamans exploit, they will do it.

So, where am I going after I die?

I have not yet made up my mind about my body. Depending on my children's wishes, I might be cremated and stuck in a plot of ground so they can visit it occasionally if they wish and remember me from a small bit of concrete evidence of my brief existence, or else I might be cremated and have my ashes scattered over the mountains where I lived, so when they see the beauty of nature every day, they can remember me until the memory fades.

I do not believe in a soul, an essence of a person's being that supposedly transcends the body and must also find a resting place after death. If such a thing as a soul exists, then why does it need some place "to go" after the body ceases to exist? If the soul is locked in to a body while the body lives, why does that body have any power while it is alive to determine the future of the soul after the body dies and frees the soul?

"Illogical," to quote another literary icon just as authentic as any other pulled out of literature to try to prove a point.

In other words, what are we to make of some religions that allow people to go through their lives proclaiming a disbelief in God, but if they become frightened of eternal damnation on their deathbeds, they can repent and say "I believe!" and God will forgive them and allow them to enter Heaven anyway?

Illogical.

Therefore, a more important question than "Where am I going?" to ask ourselves is "What influences have I made?"

I have pleased my parents while they were alive. Of course, I also disappointed them on occasion, as all children occasionally do, but in the words of someone who must have said them at least once sometime somewhere: "Nobody is perfect."

I have amused friends throughout my lifetime, which gave me pleasure as well as gave them pleasure.

I have tried to make the world a better place in which to live while I was living and I hope for others after I am dead.

I have tried to make living easier for my children while they were growing up and enabled them to mature and go out into the world on their own with a set of their own beliefs and values so that they can be happy.

I have become comfortable with my life so that I do not fear death. I live each day with the comfort of knowing that nothing is left unfinished, so that if I were to die suddenly without warning I would not be disappointed if by some so-called literal "miracle" I or my soul were to continue on in some sort of "living" existence and be able to look back or down or over or up and recognize the unfinished business.

I am comfortable.

I have tried.

I have pleased.

Most of all, I have pleased myself during my life. I kept a curious mind throughout my life so that I was always learning new things as I went from day to day and year to year and decade to decade.

I was lucky enough to be able to travel all over the world, both as a child and as an adult. I was lucky, because I believe that travel is a desirable way to obtain a world view of humanity and to learn tolerance of different customs and beliefs. Parochialism (which is a deliberate pun on my part) is self-indulgent and as destructive as a slow-growing cancer, which can destroy one's tolerance and love of humanity.

("Parochialism" is a pun, because the original meaning of "parochial" is "of or relating to a church parish," but has since come to mean "limited in scope," "narrow," and "provincial.")

At least one good thing about television is its ability to show everyone—rich and poor, young and old—what the world is like and how different all the people and wildlife all around the world are, and yet at the same time how similar we all are.

The Internet and other computer communication also help in this respect, because hating or disliking people due to their national origin or religious belief is difficult when you can talk to them directly and discuss your differences and similarities, as well as having your own prejudices pointed out to you both by the objects of your prejudices and by your peers.

I enjoyed learning. I enjoyed life.

I refused to predict anything large or anything far off in the future.

I learned to adapt to changing conditions.

I lived according to the conditions of the day, not according to the conditions of what I hoped would be the future.

I did not judge.

Who am I to try to attach my values onto someone else who had an entirely different upbringing from my own?

Who am I to believe that my values might have meaning for someone else or have guidance for others brought up in an entirely different culture from my own?

Self-discipline with everything, moderation in all.

Those are the words I have lived by, and perhaps they can be of help to others. Or perhaps not. If words or beliefs can lift the spirits of others, then so much the better. However, I will not pander to others for my own gain. That does a disservice to others and cheapens my own values and my own code of living.

Where am I going?

I am not going anywhere. I am staying right here.

Who am I?

I am that collection of material that has had a sense of self-awareness and moved through my life with a feeling of satisfaction at what I have accomplished and what I have experienced. I experience, therefore I am.

What am I doing here?

I am trying to please the ones who have made my life easier and more rewarding, as well as please myself. I am trying to make life a little easier for whomever I encounter, as well as for myself.

When will I die?

I have no idea, but I am prepared for whenever it happens.

Where am I going?

I believe I will not go anywhere. I believe I will stay right here. I am comfortable here.

I know that I will not live forever, and therefore I must be prepared for death and comfortable with the thought of death.

Aha! The secret to erasing the fear of death:

My mind is prepared for death, and I am comfortable with the thought of death, because I have lived, I have loved, I have learned, and I am ready.

CHAPTER 5

WHY Am I Here?

*"The god-men say when die we fly
Just like eaglehawk and crow."*

Imagine all of the world's problems that would disappear if everyone simply ceased to believe in God.

There would be no more religious wars. No more would groups of people believe that they were "chosen people" or else chosen by "God" to fulfill God's work on earth, and therefore they would not discriminate against other people who believe in another god or kill other people who believe the same as they do but worship a different god.

There would be no more dribble-down feelings of superiority based on how some people believe they are "closer to God" or know more about God and about God's religion and therefore those people are better and more blessed than those people who aren't and don't. All shamans would be out of business, because there would no longer be a need for them to interpret God's will for the people to whom God did not speak directly.

There would be no more intense feelings of guilt such as the following, carried around by people:

"Is God watching me?"

"Did I do the right thing according to God?"

"Will I be punished by God for this?"

"Should I do this or should I do that?"

"What does God want me to do?"

"Have I lived my life well enough according to God's teachings that I am going to go to Heaven?"

"If I do that pleasurable thing, am I really succumbing to Satan's temptations?"

Too many religious people seem to believe that atheists are either God-haters or Satanists.

"Illogical!"

To be a God-hater or a Satanist, by definition, requires a belief in God. Atheists believe that there *is* no God, and what is the point of hating something that doesn't exist?

At any rate, atheists can be just as kind and gentle, can be lovers of the Earth, of humans, and of animals, and can be peacekeepers as well as any religious person—in fact, probably more so, because too many religious people seem to be filled with hatred toward other people and fear of those people who don't believe the same way they do.

Speaking of Satan, remember that according to the mythology, Satan started out as one of God's angels, and then he broke away from God and began living independently, *just as most children do from their parents*. Perhaps the myth of Satan came about because of parents who didn't want to give up control of their children.

If everyone simply ceased to believe in God, there would be no more doubt in life, no more wondering if you are living up to someone else's standards other than your own or your immediate family's or circle of friends, no more rules set by someone you have never met, defined by people you find suspect, and believed by people with whom you don't agree.

You would be free.

Just like eaglehawk and crow.

A great deal of courage is required to admit that you have been wrong, along with a great deal of self-confidence to know that you can overcome the obstacle you have created for yourself. An even greater amount of courage and self-confidence is required to be able to renounce the existence of God and to admit to yourself that you do not believe in God anymore. You have to be able to admit that no one else is looking out for you. You have to be confident enough that you don't need any supernatural saviors to protect you from the rigors of the world. You have to have the courage to be able to make it through life on your own and not be a coward anymore and not be a member of the long line of thousands of years of millions of cowards. You have to be able to leave the comfort and safety of your parents and live independently on your own.

You have to be willing to admit that many things you were taught as a child were simply incorrect. And *wrong*.

You have to be able to live *just like eaglehawk and crow*.

Have you ever watched how baby animals react to other baby animals, ones that might even be "natural enemies"? They seem to be thrilled just to be in the presence of each other. They act as if they are in wonder of each other. They appear to be enthralled with the simple sharing of life together. They act as if they are just enjoying life and are generous in sharing that life with the other baby animals around them.

Now think about baby human beings when they are put together with other babies. They act and react the same way as the baby animals do. They couldn't care less about the other babies' sex, color, place of birth, parents' status, or, more important, parents' religion.

All the babies are like little birds, and they form natural bonds with each other to provide mutual protection against the larger dangers of life that are outside their knowledge and experience. When one baby starts crying, they all begin crying together. To them, *birds of a feather flock together* is their own kind, themselves, bonding together.

Just as baby animals grow up and eventually learn or are taught that some of their baby playmates can be either eaters or eatees, the baby humans grow up and perhaps are taught that some of their former playmates are people to be scorned or avoided or hated. However, in this case, I believe that the *birds of a feather* are the entire human race.

We are rapidly filling up the earth with ourselves. We are dangerously coming close to exhausting the earth's resources and making life even more dangerous for the existence of humankind and wildlife alike. Why, then, should we add to that danger by fighting among ourselves, by hating ourselves, and by killing ourselves? We need to get over our fear of the unknown and our hatred of people who are different. We need to grow up and leave the spiritual nest.

So, why am I here?

I believe the answer is in the existence of the animals, the *eaglehawk and crow*. Do we ever ask ourselves "Why is that dog here? Why is that cat here?"

Not unless we have such a superegotistical sense of self-importance that we believe everything else is created for our own existence and pleasure. If we ask "Why is my dog in my life?" that is one thing. "My dog is in my life, because I chose to acquire that dog and make it my pet and take care of it for the rest of its days and for my own pleasure."

However, do we ever ask "Why is that eagle here?" If we do, and if we can remove ourselves from the question, then we might be able to answer it in terms other than "Why is that eagle in my life?" because the answer to that question is "Because I chose that eagle to be in my life." I might not have caused that eagle to fly into my view and rest atop a tree before me, but I chose to contemplate its existence.

A question such as "Why is that eagle here?" or "Why am I here?" is meaningless, because the question presupposes an overall power and reason of existence that I believe simply does not exist. "That eagle is here" and "I am here" simply because we are here, we are alive, we exist.

That that is, is. That that is not, is not.

I believe that the circle of life is a *natural* circle, not a *supernatural* one. I believe that there are no forces outside of nature. I believe the only *reasons* for existence are reasons that we create for our own amusement, such as myths of creation, or create for our own knowledge, such as how two members of a species can join in a natural act of sexual commingling to create another member of their species, another baby to join the pool of babies in nature's nursery.

I believe we can learn from the animals.

I believe that we are animals:

> *Just like eaglehawk and crow.*

I believe that when human beings acquired self-knowledge and became aware that they could cope and adapt to natural, changing circumstances better than other animals could, some members of the human race began to believe that they were "better" than the other animals, they began to believe that some supernatural power "higher" in nature had either created or chosen or annointed them for that supernatural power's pleasure or for some other supernatural reason, and they began to believe that they should spend the rest of their lives worshipping that mythical supernatural power and forcing other members of their species to worship that power, as well.

I believe that when other human beings resisted worshipping the supernatural power that they had been taught they should worship, or when they worshipped another supernatural power of their own creation, they were punished and discriminated against and even killed, simply out of fear and out of the first shamans' agenda that the shamans might be wrong or might be losing the power over others they had created, and the shamans didn't want to give up that power. Once politicians—or anyone, for that matter—acquire power, they never seem to want to give up that power freely.

Religion is a self-fulfilling prophesy:

The more people I can convert to my own religion, the more legitimate my religion is.

If I can't convert people to my religion by persuasive means, I can increase my religion's numbers by killing nonbelievers of my religion.

If I am not punished for killing nonbelievers, then God must have wanted me to kill them.

If I just think *about killing people who don't believe the way I do, then God must have told me to kill them.*

I believe that we can become nature's animals again by renouncing the false belief in a supernatural power that supposedly controls both the world and the lives of the inhabitants of the world, particularly so-called *chosen* inhabitants.

What is necessary to renounce the existence of a supernatural power—in this case "God"—is a reverse "hot-stove" experiment.

When we were babies and we touched a hot stove out of curiosity, we learned that we would be hurt by touching it, and so we learned not to touch a hot stove anymore.

I thought of "God" as a stove. I didn't know whether or not that "stove" was hot. If I touched the stove of "God" tentatively and didn't get burned, then I knew that the stove isn't hot and I had no reason to fear it.

So, even though all my intellectual resources and logical training convinced me that God does not exist, I tried my reverse hot-stove experiment with some trepidation.

I said with conviction, "There is no God. He doesn't exist. God is dead. He never was. Jesus a phony, religion a buzz."

I wasn't burned by the hot stove.

Nothing happened.

I was free.

Why am I here?

I am here because I am here.

I am here because I am free.

Just like eaglehawk and crow.

CHAPTER 6

HOW Can I Be Happy?

"Might be, might be; I don't know."

What makes a religious person happy?

Supposedly the peace of mind in "knowing" that the order in the universe was created and set in motion and kept in order by "the Great Creator," "Our Father Who art in Heaven."

Be aware that when people say "I know" something, they are only saying "I believe" something very strongly.

Knowing (or believing) (or having faith) that God is keeping the universe running in good order is nothing more than the comfort that children seek from their parents in believing that the children's lives make sense and their parents will take care of them until the children are old enough and independent enough to take care of themselves, should they be strong enough and choose to do so.

Or else, religious people are happy supposedly in the relief and assurance that there is life after death and thus people can tolerate life on earth more and not fear death.

This is nothing more than the comfort that children request from their parents before going to sleep at night that all will be well and the children will wake up the next morning and thus they need not fear the darkness and the night.

In addition, remember that children and teenagers believe they are going to live forever, or, as the actor Eric Roberts once said, "The earmark of adolescence is to believe you're immortal." The converse is to know that you are going to die and to be smug and vain about "knowing" that you are going to Heaven—the earmark of a religious bore.

And supposedly religious people are happy in the comfort and peace of mind in being able to convert more people to their religion, not only because there is strength in numbers, but also because the more people who believe the way they do, the more self-fulfilling "proof" there is that their religion is the "correct" one.

This is nothing more than the comfort and relief that people feel when they are not alone—either at night or in the day—and they have the support of a group of people as they all work toward a common cause.

All religious belief seems to start with the premise of the existence of God, which comes with the absence of any proof or of any indication of proof, except for the worn, weak argument of "Well, everybody else believes, so I guess I will, too."

This can take the form of what I call the Ignorant, Refusal-to-Accept-Responsibility Argument: "Millions of people believe that God exists. Therefore, God must exist."

There is also what I call the Egotistical Argument: "I believe that God exists. Therefore, God exists."

And, finally, there is the simple Cowardly Argument: "I very much want God to exist. Therefore, God exists."

However, if there is a God and if God is so powerful as believers claim, then what is the point of people trying to prove that theirs is the "correct" religion? It either is or it isn't. If it isn't, then they lose in the end anyway. If it is, then this all-powerful God certainly doesn't need their puny efforts to acquire more converts. God can simply stage a "miracle" in order to achieve that end, assuming that such an all-powerful God would even care.

So, there is no point in trying to convert others to your belief other than for your own selfish interest in convincing yourself that you are not wrong. And you should be ashamed if you have that selfish objective in mind.

The expression "children of God" is no accident or coincidence, just as "Our Father, who art in Heaven" is no accident or coincidence. The shamans have tried throughout the history of religion to equate a mythical explanation for our adult feeling of well-being with the parents who bore us and raised us and comforted us throughout our childhood.

In other words, perhaps all of religion is nothing more than an attempt to assuage the pain of guilt we feel when we become adults and leave our parents and become independent. When families stayed together in one place and grew up together, there could have been less emphasis on a child's growing up and becoming mature in the sense of striking off and building a life of one's own. In that case, however, of a family that stayed together, a child would grow mature and take over the responsibility of the family because they were all living together. Then, as members of the family grew old and needed to be taken care of, they had their children to help take care of them.

However, if those adult children left home and created lives of their own separate from their families who had raised them, then the older members of the family could have felt a void in their lives, a need to be taken care of emotionally, if not physically. Then, a belief in God and an organized religion could have been "created" in order to comfort the old people, just as their parents had done for them decades ago. (Or, as my anthropology professor, John Greenway, might have said, religion "invented itself" because of these conditions.)

Therefore, religion and a belief in God could have been invented in order to take care of the guilt that human beings felt on leaving their parents and also to replace the comfort that the parents felt they needed when their own children left them.

Remember that in religious arguments and in atheistic arguments both, the two sides always argue from the point of believing that their position is the "true" and "correct" position:

"I believe that God exists and the world works so perfectly because God made it."

Or, "I believe that God doesn't exist and the world works so perfectly because nature works perfectly."

I don't know of any atheists who became believers in God because of someone else's religious argument, just as I don't know of any *theists* who lost their belief in God because of someone else's atheistic argument.

I believe you have to come to your own belief or lack of belief by yourself, as I did, by examining the world around you, by studying the history of mankind and the history of religions, and by deciding for yourself that the *logical* explanation for the creation of the world, the existence of humanity, and the incongruities of good, bad, right, wrong, and life itself is not that some all powerful, omniscient, spiritual "Father" created the world and its diverse human beings on one tiny planet among billions of stars for personal pleasure or reasons, but that the world all came about, and *we* came about because of the natural workings of the world itself.

Conduct an experiment. Start with the premise that God does exist, and then examine all the evidence that supports this premise. The only evidence is the word of other people, whether they are people who claim that God had chosen *them* to speak to directly or whether they are people who have no evidence other than their own simple belief in God's existence and what they were told by their parents as they grew up, just as their parents were told by their parents, and so on back for who knows how long. In addition, there are some written texts that people claim is either "the word of God" or the rules by which followers must live. Again, we have only the word of other people that this is true, and it is an extremely inefficient and risky method of acquiring followers. If God is so attentive to every detail of what goes on in the world, as claimed by the believers of God, then why doesn't God just simply appear before every person and be done with it?

On the other hand, start with the premise that God does not exist, and then examine all the evidence that supports this premise. We have scientific evidence that supports the theory that the earth is billions of years old, in contradiction to the most acclaimed written text of "the word of God," the Bible. We have hard evidence of the existence of billions of stars and galaxies, each one of which supports the theory that our puny little planet in our puny little solar system in our puny little galaxy is only one insignificant part of a tremendous whole, which doesn't speak well for the "anointed glory" of humankind. And we have direct empirical evidence of the evolution of plants and so-called "lesser" animals, as well as the hard evidence of the fossils of so-called "higher" animals that appear to be our own ancestors, which supports the theory of the evolution of mankind, which again contradicts "the word of God" that we can believe only "on faith" and because other people tell us it is true.

Many times when I have discussed religious belief with others, believers in God have set forth the challenge to prove that God doesn't exist. This exercise is impossible, because a truism in logical thought is that proving a negative premise is impossible to do. Just as you cannot prove that Santa Claus and his toy-making elves do *not* exist, you cannot prove that God, the angels, and Heaven do not exist.

However, you *can* turn the hypothesis around and put the burden of proof on those who claim that God does exist. You can either challenge them directly to prove that God exists, or else make the broader statement that all those who believe that God exists have not put forth one shred of evidence to substantiate their belief.

In other words, the most important evidence we have that God exists is that other people tell us that God exists. Given your own experience with the trustworthiness of other people, how well is that evidence likely to hold up?

The most important evidence we have that God does not exist is, again, the simple evidence of the untrustworthiness and failings of all the people who claim that God does exist. If some people tell us that God exists and has "spoken" directly to them and those people then tell us what we have to do in order to get to Heaven, and then those people are caught doing the very opposite, what does that say for the veracity of what they told us before? (And don't fall for the old cop-out excuse that humans are weak and God is strong. If God exists, why did he, she, or it make imperfect human beings in the first place? For the perverse pleasure of watching us make mistakes?)

As a mature, intelligent adult, I challenge religious believers to convince me that their so-called God did create the heavens and the earth, the creatures that fly and swim, the creatures that walk the land, and finally Adam and Eve, and then on the "seventh day" rested.

Wait a minute! If God is all-knowing, all-being, and omnipotent, why did God have to rest? Doesn't having to rest imply a failing in God? But by religious believers' definition, God can have no failings.

Okay, let us assume that God chose to rest not because God was tired, but because God wanted to give Adam and Eve and all the plants and animals a chance to get started. However, the "creationists" believe that Adam and Eve let God down when they ate the fruit from the

Tree of Knowledge (hmmm), and God kicked them out of Paradise.

Well, here is an argument that creationists could use to support their position that what they believe is correct, but one I have never heard put forward before: Assume that everything stated so far is correct. However, after Adam and Eve gained knowledge and caused God's wrath, rather than kick them out of Paradise, God left our world, left us to kill each other off in our petty little squabbles while God went off to create another world with another "Adam and Eve" who weren't so smart and would do what God wanted.

Therefore, the moral appears to be "If you want to be fat, dumb, and happy in Paradise, believe in God."

On the other hand, if you want to acquire knowledge and recognize that humans aren't perfect and acknowledge that there is death and suffering in the world, but you still want to believe in God, then believe that God created us, we let God down, and God left us. Otherwise, where is God?

So, given my position that God does not exist, how can I be happy?

Religious people might ask me how can I be happy if I believe that there is no God to take care of me, no God to take care of the world, and no God to reassure me that there is life after death.

I answer that I can be happy, because I have grown up, become an adult and become independent, and left the comfort and reassurances of my parents' home and caretaking to lead my life on my own.

In other words, if I were a bird, I have become mature enough so that I no longer need my parents to take care of me, and I have left the nest to live my life on my own, without the need for my parent birds to watch over me and without the need for an avian god of birdkind to watch over me simply because I am insecure about taking care of myself.

I can be happy when I realize that I can stop frightening myself by attributing coincidental happenings to the intervention of "God."

I learned that the chances of most anything occurring 1 time out of 4 is a very natural-occurring phenomenon. And yet many people refuse to believe in coincidence, and if that 1 chance in 4 reinforces the belief they already had in the intervention of God, they choose to reinforce their belief in God and attribute that coincidental happening to proof of God's existence.

However, whenever we cast a die and want a 6 to turn up, we probably don't believe that God intervenes (unless we are so dependent on God that we believe God intervenes in every minute detail of our lives). When we throw a 6, we probably don't believe that God blessed us with that 6, which has even greater odds of occurring at 1 in 6 than the "naturally" occurring 1 in 4. And when we roll two dice and get "snake eyes" (1 and 1) or "boxcars" (6 and 6), we probably don't believe God intervenes (unless, etc.) and punished us with that throw, which occurs at even greater odds of 1 in 36.

In other words, we choose to believe which of life's many happenstance occurrences are the result of "God's" intervention, sometimes based on whether we believe that the event is "good" or whether we believe that it is "bad."

In other words, we choose to create God in order to explain what goes on in our world, sometimes based on whether or not *we* can explain it.

Still, at times I almost catch myself believing that a coincidental occurrence can make me tend to want to believe that some *force* caused that occurrence, some supernatural power other than nature, other than natural-occurring happenstance.

We are raised to believe in a supernatural power that we call "God," and if our parents believe in God, we grow up with the idea of God shoved down our throats. It isn't until we have matured and perhaps even become independent and left our parents' household that we can begin to think for ourselves and realize that "God" was a crutch that our parents used and society uses to explain things that are merely a comfort in their own lives and for the so-called "good" of society.

I can be happy when I look at the myriads of stars and enjoy the explanation of science for the workings of nature and not confuse myself with questions of "Who made this?" or "Who created that?"

To ask those questions simply tries to elevate my own insignificant position in the universe into a vain position of believing that I—me—myself should know *everything* about the workings of the world, and if I don't, I can *explain* the workings of the world by simply saying "God made this" or "God created that."

No one "made this." No thing "created that," except for the wonderful workings of nature itself. The events of nature simply come into being because of the natural workings of themselves and the elements of nature before, around, and after them.

I can be happy with the simple existential confirmation and explanation of "Be."

I am, because I am. I need no other explanation.

I am happy sometimes, because sometimes I simply choose to be happy.

I have discovered how I can create my own feelings of happiness and sadness. Once, I was unhappy with how a love affair was progressing, and I realized that I had started to feel sorry for myself, started making myself more unhappy, and was dangerously approaching a severe state of depression. I consciously stopped the downward spiral of depression and forced myself to return to a state of calm. I realized that I had control over my own feelings and didn't need someone else or some thing else to make me either happy or sad.

I am happy other times, because sometimes I simply observe nature and enjoy its natural wonder and intricate workings. I live at the conjunction of the plains and the mountains, and I live a peaceful, calm existence. I can see the stars at night with no trouble. I can watch the moon sneak over a ridge with delight. I have mule deer who come around regularly, and I enjoy watching them play or rest on my property. Many times, two 4-by-4-point stags sit beneath my kitchen window for at least half an hour at a time appearing to watch the traffic drive by 50 yards below them. Once I was on my deck one evening when a doe must have just given birth to a fawn behind my house, and I observed the mother deer teaching her newborn baby how to walk for the first time as she led the fawn around my property in the fading light. Many times I will be sitting at my desk writing, and I will look out the window and see a deer sit beneath a tree to rest and take comfort of the shade.

There will be times in the morning when I walk down to the road to get the papers, and a group of deer will be between me and the mailbox. I will calmly walk right by them, talking to them in a soft, gentle voice, and they will just glance at me and keep on eating as we all go on about our lives in harmony.

In the summer, I keep a large hummingbird feeder in the pine tree just outside the window in front of my desk, and I can tell when at least three different hummingbirds appear to take up residence in that tree near the feeder. I recognize the individual hummingbirds, and I watch them play around the feeder with each other and rest in the tree trying to contain their nervous energy. I take the feeder indoors at night to prevent badgers and squirrels from sucking it dry overnight, and in the morning when I take the feeder out, the hummingbirds are waiting for breakfast, humming and throbbing around my head while I hang the feeder back up in the tree.

I have seen a red fox scamper up my driveway early in the morning looking for food, another one trot across my property in the afternoon keeping a wary eye out for trouble, and a black fox slink away late in the afternoon. I have watched an eagle sitting majestically at the top of a pine tree just 25 yards away from my house. I have heard coyotes howling their delight at the full moon above us, and when I have walked outside, I could smell their pungent odor across the road.

I am happy just being a part of nature and one of the many animals and all the other life forms around me. I believe that we need to be around animals so that we don't convince ourselves that we are "chosen" and "blessed" merely by our existence. I believe that we are only one species in a wealth of life forms and we are all equal in importance in our struggles for our place and existence on the planet.

Consequently, I take notice of all other life forms that share my property with me, whether they are bears, deer, foxes, coyotes, eagles, hawks, crows, magpies, robins, woodpeckers, Downy Woodpeckers, Brewer's Blackbirds, Wilson's Warblers, Pigmy Nuthatches, starlings, Sparrow Hawks, pigeons, meadowlarks, blue jays, Steller's Jays, Smith's Longspurs, chimney swifts, hummingbirds, raccoons, badgers, brown squirrels, black squirrels, a prairie dog, skunks, bats, voles, mice, snakes, butterflies, dragonflies, moths, caterpillars, slugs, earthworms, grasshoppers, praying mantises, crickets, spiders, ticks, hornets, wasps, yellowjackets, bees, honeybees, bumblebees, ant lions, black ants, red ants, ladybugs, doodlebugs, stinkbugs, horseflies, houseflies, mosquitoes, or gnats.

Those are just the ones that I have seen on or around my property. Although I haven't seen any mountain lions or moose myself, I know that they are also in the area. I believe that we should all strive to live together with all the animals instead of being so egotistical that we try to eradicate anything we don't like or that we believe is a nuisance to us and our preferred way of living.

My heart was broken when I heard a quote from Frank H. Mayer, a buffalo hunter of the 1800s: "The buffalo was gone. Maybe we served our purpose in helping abolish the buffalo. Maybe it was our ruthless harvesting of him which telescoped the control of the Indian by a decade or maybe more. Or maybe I'm just rationalizing. Maybe we were just a greedy lot who wanted to get ours and to hell with posterity, the buffalo, or anyone else, just so we kept our scalps on and our money pouches filled. I think maybe that was the way it was."

How many other tragedies have occurred throughout the history of humanity simply because of the attitude, "We . . . wanted to get ours and to hell with posterity . . . or anyone else"?

I can be happy when I can set aside any anger or resentment that for the greater part of my life I have been fooled and tricked by religious shamans who have led people to believe that only the shamans know the meaning of life and if people would just follow the teachings of the shamans and believe what the charlatans told them to believe, then the people would have inner peace on earth and be assured of having everlasting "life" after death—just as parents reassure their children that the night is not to be feared and the children will wake up tomorrow and all is right with the world.

I can be happy, if I *must* believe in some spiritual guidance, in accepting the wonderful spiritual happiness of nature and in relishing the wonder of being alive, of enjoying simple existence, of *being*.

I can be happy when I no longer fear death, because I have enjoyed my life.

I can be happy when I realize there is no such thing as "good" and "evil" or "right" and "wrong" outside of what is desirable for all humanity's existence and perpetuation, for the existence and perpetuation of all living things, and outside of not following the simple Ten Disciplines:

1. The Earth is my home, which has brought me to life out of the elements of itself.
2. I shall worship no other spirit than the Earth, nor shall I damage the Earth.
3. I shall take time off occasionally for myself.
4. I shall work hard when necessary and play hard when possible.
5. I shall be kind to everyone and to every thing.
6. I shall not kill anything or anyone out of hatred or for personal gain, even when ordered to do so.
7. I shall be prudent in my choice of lovers.
8. I shall not take what does not belong to me.
9. I shall be honest to others and to myself.
10. I shall treat others the way I want them to treat me.

I can be happy when I don't ask "why?"

People who ask "why" and get upset over life's so-called tragedies believe that "God" made order in the world and therefore God should be watching out for them and taking care of them and that order, just as their parents did for them when they were children. Thus, when one of life's "tragedies" occurs, those people's sense of order and comfort of being taken care of by their "Father in Heaven" is thrown out of kilter, they become upset and confused, and they become angry because they feel that they have been betrayed, just as they probably became angry as children when something their parents had promised them didn't come true.

If you don't believe in God, then you don't need to know "why."

Things happen and you aren't betrayed when "bad" things happen, just as you aren't blessed when so-called "good" things happen, because all things good and bad carry the same weight. Good things happen because of "luck," the 1 chance out of 4 that you choose good things to be. Bad things happen because of "bad luck," either the same 1 chance out of 4 that you choose to identify as bad luck or the 3 chances out of 4 that you choose to associate with an unlucky life.

You can rest easier if you believe there is no God. I know, because I began to rest much easier after I stopped believing in the existence of God.

I am happy when I observe the "innocent" natural animals around me, when I observe the inexperienced babies simply enjoying life as it has been given them, simply enjoying their own existence, and I can identify with *them* rather than with some meanspirited, egotistical, supercilious, angry, frightened, "better-than-thou" and "holier-than-thou," religious, "God-fearing" adults who try to convince me that I should abandon my own belief and convert to their illogical belief, simply because they claim to have millions of similar believers, thousands of years of history, and a written text of dubious origin to guide them.

I am happy when I practice my code of self-discipline with everything, moderation in all.

I am happy when I have a sense of humor, a love and respect of nature, a respect for humanity, control of my appetites, and a stimulation of my senses, as well as a continual exercise of my creative abilities.

I create; therefore I am.

I am, because I am.

I am happy, because I don't need an explanation for everything. Some things just *are*.

I am happy when I refrain from telling other people how I believe *they* should live.

I am happy when I learn or discover new information about the world, about people, and about me.

I am happy when I can please others, as well as please myself.

I am happy, because I don't need false, empty reassurances that "all is right with the world," that everything has a purpose, and that I will be taken care of throughout my life and illogically even after my death by some supernatural power that I am supposed to believe in without any evidence other than the word of other people.

I am happy, because I don't need a supernatural explanation of everything that occurs and everything that is "out there," whether it be the stars or tosses of dice or ghosts or UFOs or witches or anything supernatural or paranormal or . . . God.

I am happy, because I don't worship children, just as I don't worship God, and I don't put children's needs and comfort and happiness over the needs and comfort and happiness of adults.

I am happy with what I have, and I do not believe that I would be exponentially happier than I am now if I had more than I have now.

I am happy, because I can answer the questions "Who am I," "What do I believe," "When will I die," "Where am I going," "Why am I here," and "How can I be happy," which I have done in this book.

I am happy, because I do not feel "betrayed" when someone close to me dies or when someone I have loved from afar ceases to exist.

I am happy, because I do not need to believe in a god to take care of me or in a supernatural being to allow me to be happy or to make me be happy.

I am happy, because I have proven my existence to my own satisfaction:

I have grown independent of my beginnings and of my parents.

I have been loved.

I have loved.

I have perpetuated my own existence by helping in the creation of two more creatures on this earth and of this earth, my children.

I have not hated.

I have not broken the Ten Disciplines.

I am happy.

I continue to be happy.

I am.

I be.

Who am I? I am one person in a world of many diverse peoples with many diverse cultures and diverse religions, as well as one person in a world of many diverse life forms, all struggling to maintain a peaceful coexistence on one tiny plot of spherical ground and water within a myriad of other worlds.

What do I believe? I believe that the concept of "God" is the Santa Claus myth for adults, perpetuated by an illogical fear of death by the believers and a self-serving desire to perpetuate that myth by the shamans.

When will I die? I will die when my body exhausts itself or when I am unlucky enough to experience an unforeseen accident, and I am not afraid.

Where am I going? After I die, my body will decompose either quickly through cremation or slowly in the ground through natural processes.

Why am I here? I am here, because the natural process of evolution brought me to life with the help of my parents, and I was lucky enough to be able to live to adulthood and independence.

How can I be happy? I am happy, because I observe the world around me and am comfortable with my place in that world and also because I choose to be happy.

I am me, I am myself, and I am I, simply because I am.

CHAPTER 7

My Road to Atheism

I was born in Carmel, California. Because my father was in the Army, I moved considerably with my family, and before I was 10, I had lived in the following locations in the following order:

1. Monterey, California
2. Medford, Oregon
3. Lawton, Oklahoma
4. Pampa, Texas
5. Lawton, Oklahoma (a second time)
6. Minot, North Dakota
7. El Paso, Texas
8. Tacoma, Washington
9. Kennewick, Washington
10. Erlangen, Germany

My parents were Protestants, and in those days when we lived on an Army base, we had a choice of three religious services to attend whenever we wanted: Catholic, Jewish, or Protestant.

After living three years in Germany—the longest amount of time I had ever spent in one place—my family and I moved back to the United States and to Lebanon, Missouri.

While living in Lebanon, I became baptized at 13, simply because my best friend was going to be baptized in the Southern Baptist Church, which my parents and my brother and I also attended.

At that age, I already had doubts about the existence of God, which I verbalized as "God probably doesn't really exist, but if I ever have children, it might be a good thing to teach them about God and let them believe in God until they grow older and can decide for themselves."

While sitting in the front pew next to my best friend along with the rest of the people waiting to be baptized, as the Southern Baptist preacher stood before the congregation and preached about Fire and Brimstone, I noticed that my best friend was crying, and I thought, "Whoa! Something strange is going on here." And then as the curtains were opened to reveal the huge baptismal tank filled with water behind the preacher, I became convinced that something even stranger was going on. Up until then, I had believed that being baptized consisted of a basin of water and a damp forehead.

When my time came, I had already watched my friend become "saved," and I was prepared for the experience of being totally immersed in the waters of the tank. Even so, I was shocked when the preacher suddenly grabbed my mouth and the back of my head and plunged me into the cold water and held me under, which symbolized that the preacher—the shaman—literally held the life and death of the person being baptized in his hands.

However, I became even less convinced in the reality of God, and when the following year my family and I then moved to Colorado Springs, Colorado, where my father retired from the Army, I attended the First Christian Church with my parents only reluctantly, even though they always pressured me to go with them.

I lived in Colorado Springs for five years before leaving home and moving to Boulder, Colorado, to attend the University of Colorado on journalism and National Merit scholarships, where I received a B.A. degree in English literature in the honors program, graduating Phi Beta Kappa, and where in one psychology class my I.Q. was tested to be 160.

Whenever I returned "home" to visit my parents during my years at college, I was able to avoid hurting my parents' feelings and having to inform them that I did not believe what they believed and that I did not believe in God and I was not going to accompany them to church on Sunday, because I had "forgotten" to bring my suit home with me. I had become independent, I had left home, and I had left the nest, *just like eaglehawk and crow.*

During the course of four years of college, I studied the following subjects:

First Year: Fall Semester
    Advanced Freshman English (English Language)
    Introduction to Literature (English Literature)
    General Psychology (Psychology)
    History of Western Civilization (History)
    Physical Education (Physical Education)
    Introduction to Journalism (Journalism)

First Year: Spring Semester
    Physical Education (Physical Education)
    Advanced Freshman English (English Language)
    Introduction to Literature (English Literature)
    History of Western Civilization (History)
    Problems of American History (Honors)
    General Psychology (Psychology)

Second Year: Fall Semester
    Physical Geography—Weather and Climate (Geography)
    Beginning French (French)
    Second Year Composition (English Language)
    Classic Social Theories (Philosophy)
    Survey of English Literature (English Literature)

Second Year: Spring Semester
    Survey of English Literature (English Literature)
    Physical Geography—Geomorphology (Geography)
    Beginning French (French)
    Second Year Composition (English Language)
    Modern Social Theories (Philosophy)

Third Year: Fall Semester
    History of English Language (English Language)
    Second Year Reading and Conversation (French)
    American Literature (English Literature)
    Development of the English Novel (English Literature)
    Shakespeare (English Literature)
    American Novel (English Literature)

Third Year: Spring Semester
    Principles of Anthropology (Anthropology)
    American Literature (English Literature)
    Development of British Drama (English Literature)
    American Novel (English Literature)
    Shakespeare (English Literature)

Fourth Year: Fall Semester
    Greek & Roman Epic Translations (Classics)
    Phonetics (Speech)
    Origins & Development of Religion (Anthropology)
    Early American Frontier (History)
    Oral Interpretation of Literature (Speech)
    History of Philosophy (Philosophy)

Fourth Year: Spring Semester
    Ancient History (Classics)
    Later Victorians (English Literature)
    Greek Tragedy (Classics)
    Primitive Literature (Anthropology)
    Later American Frontier (History)
    Primitive Arts & Crafts (Anthropology)
    Social Organization (Anthropology)

The mixture of anthropology, classics, and philosophy classes continued to lead the way to my further doubt in the existence of God, but my studies in the "Origins & Development of Religion" convinced me.

If there was a God, why would that God have created so many different religions, some with the same or similar mythologies, with so many different followers, all believing so fanatically that their God was the one true God that they were even willing to kill the followers of a different religion in the name of God?

Illogical.

If there were more than one god, why would those gods allow their followers to kill each other off in the name of the gods when the gods themselves must be in a peaceful coexistence with one another?

Illogical.

If the purpose of life is to worship the one true God and after death have life everlasting in Heaven, why would the one true God allow and even condone the mass hate and destruction of people who were unlucky enough to be born to parents who believed in a different "one true God"?

Illogical.

If there is one true God, why did so many different people evolve in the world creating different myths, many of which contain the same details as the myths of other religions?

Because they were misguided in their worship of the one true God?

Illogical.

Because there is no God and they were simply following the worldwide desire of having someone or some thing take care of them after their parents no longer could?

Logical.

Because they were afraid to be independent and on their own, because they desired that death be no more than the nightly darkness, and because they required the reassurance of each dawn that succeeded each night?

Logical.

The idea of God is no more than *in loco parentis* (in the place of a parent) for all adults, which is what my university claimed to be for its students.

Just as I left my parents and the comfort of my parents' home to attend college, and just as I was graduated from college with the knowledge of philosophy and classics and anthropology and religion and history and literature, I also graduated from the necessity of the comfort of a belief in God, and it was no more traumatic than when I lost my belief in Santa Claus.

And that is why I am an atheist.

BIBLIOGRAPHY

The following works collectively contributed to the conclusion by the author that there is no God:

Attenborough, David. *Life on Earth: A Natural History*. Boston: Little, Brown and Company, 1979.

Bernard, Abbot of Clairvaux. *The Steps of Humility*. Translated by George Bosworth Burch. Notre Dame, Indiana: University of Notre Dame Press, 1963.

Blyth, R.H. *Zen and Zen Classics*. New York: Vintage Books, 1978.

Boethius, Anacius Manlius Severinus. *The Consolation of Philosophy*. New York: The Bobbs-Merrill Company, Inc., 1962.

Bulfinch, Thomas. *Myths of Greece and Rome*. New York: Penguin Books, 1981.

Ceram, C.W. *Gods, Graves, and Scholars/The Story of Archaeology*. New York: Alfred A. Knopf, Inc., 1952.

Chapman, Graham; Cleese, John; Gilliam, Terry; Idle, Eric; Jones, Terry; and Palin, Michael. *Monty Python's The Life of Brian (Of Nazareth)*. New York: Ace Books, 1979.

Clark, Kenneth. *A Guide to Civilization*. New York: Time Inc., 1970.

Cousteau, Jacques-Yves, and the Staff of the Cousteau Society. *The Cousteau Almanac: An Inventory of Life on Our Water Planet*. New York: Dolphin Books, 1981.

Cousteau, Jacques-Yves. *The Ocean World of Jacques Cousteau: Volume 1: Oasis in Space*. U.S.A.: The World Publishing Company, 1973.

Cousteau, Jacques-Yves. *The Silent World*. New York: Ballantine Books, 1973.

Cudmore, L.L. Larison. *The Center of Life: A Natural History of the Cell*. New York: Quadrangle/The New York Times Book Company, Inc., 1977.

De Waal, Frans. *Good Natured: The Origins of Right and Wrong in Humans and Other Animals*. New York: Harvard University Press, 1996.

DeMott, Benjamin. *Supergrow: Essays and Reports on Imagination in America*. New York: E. P. Dutton & Co., Inc., 1969.

Descartes, Rene. *Meditations on First Philosophy*. Translated by Laurence J. Lafleur. 2d ed. New York: The Liberal Arts Press, Inc., 1960.

Evans, Bergen. *The Natural History of Nonsense*. New York: Vintage Books, 1960.

Fast, Howard. *Time and the Riddle: Thirty-One Zen Stories*. Boston: Houghton Mifflin Company, 1975.

Ferris, Anthony R., ed. *Spiritual Sayings of Kahlil Gibran*. New York: The Citadel Press, 1962.

Fiedler, Leslie A. *No! In Thunder/Essays on Myth and Literature*. Boston: Beacon Press, 1960.

Frazer, James G. *The Golden Bough/The Roots of Religion and Folklore*. New York: Avenel Books, 1981.

Frazer, Sir James George. *The New Golden Bough*. Edited by Theodor H. Gaster. New York: Anchor Books, 1961.

Gamow, George. *One Two Three . . . Infinity: Facts and Speculations of Science*. New York: Bantam Books, 1947, 1961.

Ghiselin, Brewster, ed. *The Creative Process: A Symposium*. New York: The New American Library, 1952.

Gibran, Kahlil. *The Prophet*. New York: Quality Paperbook Book Club, 1995.

The Gideons International. *Holy Bible*. U.S.A.: National Publishing Company, 1978.

Greenway, John. *Down Among the Wild Men: The Narrative Journal of Fifteen Years Pursuing the Old Stone*

Age Aborigines of Australia's Western Desert. Boston: Little, Brown and Company, 1972.

Greenway, John. *The Inevitable Americans*. New York: Alfred A. Knopf, 1964.

Greenway, John. *Literature Among the Primitives*. Pennsylvania: Folklore Associates, Inc., 1964.

Hofstadter, Douglas R. *Metamagical Themas: Questing for the Essence of Mind and Pattern*. New York: Basic Books, Inc., 1985.

James, William. *Selected Papers on Philosophy*. New York: E.P. Dutton & Co., 1961.

Kant, Immanuel. *Foundations of the Metaphysics of Morals: And What Is Enlightenment?* New York: The Bobbs-Merrill Company, Inc., 1959.

Keen, Sam, and Fox, Anne Valley. *Telling Your Story: A Guide to Who You Are and Who You Can Be*. New York: Doubleday & Company, Inc., 1973.

Kroeber, A.L. *Anthropology: Culture Patterns & Processes*. New York: Harbinger Books, 1963.

Metzger, Bruce M., and Coogan, Michael D., ed. *The Oxford Companion to the Bible*. New York: Harvard University Press, 1993.

Minsky, Marvin. *The Society of Mind*. New York: Simon and Schuster, 1985.

Musashi, Miyamoto; Victor Harris, trans. *A Book of Five Rings*. Woodstock, New York: The Overlook Press, 1974.

Neihardt, John G. *Black Elk Speaks: Being the Life Story of a Holy Man of the Oglala Sioux*. Lincoln, Nebraska: University of Nebraska Press, 1961.

Ortega Y Gasset, Jose. *The Dehumanization of Art: And Other Writings on Art and Culture*. 3d ed. New York: Doubleday Anchor Books, 1952.

Panati, Charles. *Panati's Extraordinary Endings of Practically Everything and Everybody*. New York: Harper & Row, Publishers, 1989.

Pelikan, Jaroslav, ed. *The World Treasure of Modern Religious Thought*. Boston: Little, Brown and Company, 1990.

Raglan, Lord. *The Hero: A Study in Tradition, Myth, and Drama*. New York: Vintage Books, 1956.

Rexroth, Kenneth. *Classics Revisited*. New York: New Directions Publishing Corporation, 1986.

Reynolds, David K. *Playing Ball on Running Water: The Japanese Way for Building a Better Life*. New York: William Morrow and Company, Inc., 1984.

Seabury, David. *The Art of Selfishness*. New York: Cornerstone Library, 1937, 1964.

Senzaki, Nyogen, and McCandless, Ruth Stout. *Buddhism and Zen*. New York: The Wisdom Library, 1953.

Service, Elman R. *A Profile of Primitive Culture*. New York: Harper & Brothers, Publishers, 1958.

Smith, Homer W. *Man and His Gods*. New York: Universal Library, 1952.

Smith, Joseph, trans. *The Book of Mormon*. Utah: The Church of Jesus Christ of Latter-Day Saints, 1981.

Teter, D. Park. *Revolution Against War*. Ahmeek, Michigan: Adventures in Reality, 1991.

Thomas, Lewis. *Late Night Thoughts on Listening to Mahler's Ninth Symphony*. New York: Bantam Books, 1984.

Thomas, Lewis. *The Lives of a Cell: Notes of a Biology Watcher*. New York: The Viking Press, 1974.

Thomas, Lewis. *The Medusa and the Snail: More Notes of a Biology Watcher*. New York: The Viking Press, 1979.

Thomson, J.A.K., trans. *The Ethics of Aristotle*. Baltimore, Maryland: Penguin Books, 1955.

Von Daniken, Erich. *Chariots of the Gods?* New York: Bantam Books, 1968.

Von Daniken, Erich. *Gods from Outer Space*. New York: Bantam Books, 1968.

Watts, Alan W. *The Meaning of Happiness: The Quest for Freedom of the Spirit in Modern Psychology and the Wisdom of the East.* New York: Perennial Library, 1940, 1968.

The Wisdom of Confucius. Mount Vernon, N.Y.: The Peter Pauper Press, 1963.

Wolfe, W. Thomas. *And the Sun Is Up: Kundalini Rises in the West.* Red Hook, N.Y.: Academy Hill Press, 1978.

Wood, Ernest. *Yoga.* Baltimore, Maryland: Penguin Books, Inc., 1959.

Worcester, Philip G. *A Textbook of Geomorphology.* 2d ed. New York: D. Van Norstrand Company, Inc., 1948.

Yogi, Maharishi Mahesh. *The Science of Being and Art of Living.* New York: Signet Books, 1968.

Zen Buddhism. Mount Vernon, N.Y.: The Peter Pauper Press, 1959.

INDEX

aboriginal Australian poem 33, 45
abortion 37
Africa 11
Ahab, King 10
all, moderation in 29, 47, 52
animals, baby 58, 59
Apollo 9
Arapahoe Indians 46
Argonauts 10
arguments, atheistic 69
arguments, religious 69
Arthur, King 9
Asclepius 9
atheistic arguments 69
Athenian hero 12
author's background 87
Australian poem, aboriginal 33, 45

babies 58, 59, 61, 63, 82
baby animals 58, 59
Baptist church, Southern 88
begotten 35

Bellerophone 10
betrayal, feeling of 81, 84
Bible 10, 16, 29, 30, 35, 70, 97, 98
    Deuteronomy, book of 29, 30
    Exodus, book of 29, 30
    Genesis, book of 16
    John, book of 34-36
    Old Testament 10
Biblical prophets 11
Bibliography 95
"birds of a feather flock together" 59
books of Bible
    Deuteronomy 29, 30
    Exodus 29, 30
    Genesis 16
    John 34-36
"boxcars" 75
Burns, Robert 27

Catholic church 87
Celtic hero 11
charlatans 80
children 65, 66, 68, 69, 80, 81, 85, 88
    worship of 84
children of God 67
Chimera 10
Christ, Jesus 12, 14, 15, 25, 33, 36, 63, 100
Christian missionaries 34
Christmas, religion of 13-15
churches 88, 89, 100
circle of life 60
Claus, Santa 13-18, 71, 85, 93
coat of many colors 10

coincidence 39, 67, 68, 74
Colorado, University of 89
colors, coat of many 10
Commandments, Ten 29, 30
common events in lives of traditional folk heroes 8
Complex, Oedipus 11

dance, ghost 46, 47
death
    fear of 34, 36-39, 43, 48, 49, 53, 66, 80, 85
    life after 23, 37, 38, 45, 66, 73, 80, 92
Demeter 11
Deuteronomy, book of 29, 30
dice 75, 83
Dionysus 10
Disciplines, Ten 30, 81, 85
dribble-down feelings of superiority 55

eaglehawk and crow 33, 55, 57-59, 61, 63, 89
earth's resources, exhaustion of 59
Egypt 10
Elijah 10
English, pidgin 33
English hero 11
events, common, in lives of traditional folk heroes 8
everlasting life 35-37
everything, self-discipline with 52, 82
exhaustion of earth's resources 59
Exodus, book of 29, 30
experiment, reverse "hot-stove" 62, 63
explanations, supernatural 83
"eyes, snake" 75

fear of death 34, 36-39, 43, 48, 49, 53, 66, 80, 85
fear and hatred 24
feeling of betrayal 81, 84
feelings of superiority, dribble-down 55
First Christian church 89
Fitzgerald, F. Scott 28
Fleece, Golden 10
folk hero, Javanese 12
folk heroes, traditional, common events in lives of 8
folk tale, generic hero 8
football, professional 34
"For God so loved the world" 35
Forest, Sherwood 11

Gaea 47
Gates, Pearly 33, 45
generic hero folk tale 8
Genesis, book of 16
German hero 12
Germanic mythology 12
ghost dance 46, 47
ghost shirts 46, 47
ghosts 83
God, children of 67
"God told me to do it" 22
god-men say 33, 45, 55
"God's will" 56
gods, Olympian 9
Golden Fleece 10
Greek heroes 10
Greek mythology 9-12
Gunung, Watu 12

Hades 12
Hamlet 46
happiness
    for the author 76, 80, 84
    for a religious person 65
Harney, William 33
hatred, fear and 24
Heaven 12, 17, 23, 33, 36, 37, 40, 45-47, 49, 56, 65-67, 71, 72, 81, 92
Hercules 10, 12
hero
    Athenian 12
    Celtic 11
    English 11
    folk tale, generic 8
    German 12
    Greek 10
    Javanese 12
    Shiluk 11
Hero, The 8
heroes, traditional folk, common events in lives of 8
Hood, Robin 11
"hot-stove" experiment, reverse 62, 63
How Can I Be Happy? 65, 73, 86
hubris 26
humor, sense of 83

in loco parentis 93
Indians
    Arapahoe 46
    Paiute 46
    Sioux 47

influences 49
Internet 51

Jacob 10
Jason 10
Javanese folk hero 12
Jesus Christ 12, 14, 15, 25, 33, 36, 63, 100
Jewish religion 87
John, book of 34-36
"John 3:16" 34, 36
Joseph 10

King Ahab 10
King Arthur 9

life
    circle of 60
    everlasting 35-37
    meaning of 80
life after death 23, 37, 38, 45, 66, 73, 80, 92
Llawgyffes, Llew 11
Lord Raglan 8, 9, 12
luck 82

"Man Was Made to Mourn" 27
many colors, coat of 10
massacre at Wounded Knee 47
meaning of life 80
Medusa 11
messianic movements 45, 46
might be, might be; I don't know 33, 43, 65
Minotaur 12
missionaries, Christian 34

moderation in all 29, 47, 52, 82
Moses 11, 30
Mount Olympus 10, 12
Mount Sinai 30
"Mourn, Man Was Made to" 27
movements, messianic 45, 46
My Road to Atheism 87
mythology
    Germanic 12
    Greek 9-12
myths 8, 15, 60, 92

nature 48, 60, 61, 69, 75-78, 80, 83
nest, spiritual 59
Nicholas, Saint 15
Niebelungen 12
Nile, Upper 11
"Nobody is perfect" 49
North Pole 13, 15
Nyikang 11

Oedipus 11, 12
Oedipus Complex 11
Old Testament 10
Olympian gods 9
Olympus, Mount 10, 12

Paiute Indians 46
parentis, in loco 93
"Peace, Rest In" 39
Pearly Gates 33, 45
Pegasus 10
Peloponnesus 11

Pelops 11
"perfect, nobody is" 49
Perseus 11
Pharaoh 11
pidgin English 33
poem, aboriginal Australian 33, 45
pogroms 21
Pole, North 13, 15
predictions 45, 46
professional football 34
prophets, Biblical 11
Protestant church 87

Rachel 10
Raglan, Lord 8, 9, 12
raglan sleeve 8
religion of Christmas 13-15
religious arguments 69
religious wars 55
Remus 12
resources, earth's, exhaustion of 59
"Rest In Peace" 39
reverse "hot stove" experiment 62, 63
riddle of Sphinx 11
R.I.P. 39
Robin Hood 11
Rome 12
Romulus 12

Saint Nicholas 15
Santa Claus 13-18, 71, 85, 93
Satan 36, 56, 57
self-discipline with everything 52, 82

sense of humor 83
Shakespeare 46
shamans 13, 16, 34, 36, 38, 47, 48, 55, 62, 68, 80, 85, 89
Sherwood Forest 11
Shiluk hero 11
shirts, ghost 46, 47
"Should not perish, but have everlasting Life" 35, 36
Siegfried 12
Sigurd 12
Sinai, Mount 30
Sioux Indians 48
sleeve, raglan 8
"snake eyes" 75
soul 48, 50
Southern Baptist church 88
Sphinx, riddle of 11
spiritual nest 59
suicide 37
superiority, dribble-down feelings of 55
supernatural explanations 83

television 50
Ten Commandments 29, 30
Ten Disciplines 30, 81, 85
Testament, Old 10
"That he gave his only begotten Son" 35
"That whosoever believeth in him" 35
Theseus 12
tolerance 50
traditional folk heroes, common events in lives of 8
travel, world 50

UFOs 83
University of Colorado 89
Upper Nile 11

Volsungasaga 12

wars, religious 55
Watu Gunung 12
What am I doing here? 52
What Do I Believe? 21, 24, 85
When Will I Die? 33, 39, 52, 85
Where Am I Going? 45, 49, 52, 53, 86
Who Am I? 7, 15, 52, 85
Why Am I Here? 55, 59, 60, 63, 86
"will, God's" 56
witches 83
"word of God" 70, 71
world travel 50
worship of children 84
Wounded Knee, massacre at 47
Wovoka 46, 47

Zeus 9-12